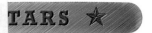

BRIANA SCURRY
SUPER SAVER

BY MARK STEWART

Ne⌐   ⌐y.

Danbury, Connecticut

Photo Credits

Photographs ©: Allsport USA: 24 (Brian Bahr), 23, 27 (David Cannon), 47 (Otto Greule), 40 (Vincent Laforet), 21 (Rick Stewart), 20; AP/Wide World Photos: 43 (Lynsey Addario), 41 (Michael Caulfield), 31 (Doug Mills), 37 (Eric Risberg), 32 (Paul Sakuma); Corbis-Bettmann: 10, 38, 44 right (AFP); International Sports Images: cover, 3, 6, 13, 18, 28, 45, 46 (J. Brett Whitesell); University of Massachusetts, Media Relations: 17, 44 left.

Visit Children's Press® on the Internet at:
http://publishing.grolier.com

Library of Congress Cataloging-in-Publication Data

Stewart, Mark.
    Briana Scurry, super saver / by Mark Stewart.
      p. cm. — (Sports stars)
    Summary: A biography of the team USA soccer goalie from her childhood to the 1999 Women's World Cup championship.
      ISBN 0-516-22045-4 (lib. bdg.)   0-516-27070-2 (pbk.)
      1. Scurry, Briana, 1971---Juvenile literature. 2. Soccer players—United States—Biography—Juvenile literature. [1. Scurry, Briana, 1971- 2. Soccer players. 3. Afro-Americans—Biography. 4. Women—Biography.] I. Title: Briana Scurry. II. Title. III. Series.

GV942.7.S37 S74   2000
796.334'092—dc21
[B]

                                      00-020807

★ CONTENTS ★

★ 1 ★

CALL HER "THE WALL"

Briana Scurry's eyes widen as an enemy player surrounds a loose ball, slices past a defender, and begins to angle toward the goal. As her teammates move toward the intruder, Briana spots two other opponents crisscrossing in front of the penalty box. Team USA is in trouble.

Briana makes a sudden move in the direction of the dribbler, who quickly crosses the ball to the other side of the field. In one swift motion, the player receiving the pass controls it and curls a shot toward the top corner of the goal. Nine times out of ten, this is an automatic goal. But not with Briana in the net.

Like a superhero swooping in to save the day, she springs across the goalmouth, stretches her arm toward the ball, and tips it over the bar. The crowd goes crazy while Briana picks herself up and prepares for the next play.

She may be wearing her "game face," but inside she is laughing. Her "miracle" save was really no miracle. Briana had tricked the first player into passing and was already moving toward the second player's shot before the ball even touched her foot.

It should be against the rules to have a goalkeeper this good. There was no way that ball was going in. No way at all.

★ 2 ★

ALL-AROUND ATHLETE

Many places in the United States are
considered to be soccer "hotbeds"
today, but Dayton, Minnesota—a suburb of
Minneapolis—is not really one of them. Although
Briana Scurry was born there in 1971, Dayton is
more of a football and hockey town. Perhaps that
is why Briana did not even think about playing
soccer until she was 11 years old.

None of Briana's eight older brothers and
sisters thought much of the game, and her
parents understood almost nothing about it.
But everyone in the Scurry family was well
aware that young "Bri" was a very special girl

When Briana first took up soccer, she played on a boys' team. Her coach put her in goal for her own "safety."

with a very special knack for sports. "I was hooked on sports pretty early," confirms Briana, who was one of the best in her class at basketball and floor hockey before she ever encountered a soccer ball.

From what Briana had seen, soccer seemed like a real challenge. So she asked to join one of the teams in Dayton. At that time, the town did not have a girls' soccer league, so Briana was placed on a boy's team. "The coach put me in goal because he thought I would be safer there," she remembers.

The following year, Dayton set up a girls'
league. Because soccer was new to so many of
the players, the games were often disorganized.
Briana would stand in the goalmouth waiting for
a shot to come her way, but the opportunities to
make plays were few and far between. Bored and
frustrated, Briana asked to play on the forward
line. Over the next three years, Briana was her
team's best scorer.

After awhile, Briana found that she missed
her goalie position. She remembered how much
fun it was to make a diving save, to throw a pass
that started a rush, and to kick the ball way over
the heads of her opponents. "I realized I could
control the game from the goal," Briana says.
Finally, she asked to switch back.

Briana enrolled at Anoka High School in 1986.
During her years there, she blossomed into a
terrific all-around athlete. She played soccer in
the fall, basketball in the winter, and competed

on the softball and track teams during the spring. Her best sport, by far, was basketball. She was an All-State player with lightning-fast hands, and legs like steel coils. "I had mad hops," she laughs. Indeed, her vertical jump was once measured at 27 inches!

These were the same skills Briana used to become a top goalkeeper. She loved to launch her body through the air and deflect shots past the goalpost or over the bar. And she enjoyed watching the effect on the other team when she made a spectacular save. "My high-school coach used to say I was long on athleticism and short on technique."

From her days as a forward, Briana had an idea of how shooters think and she used this knowledge with great creativity. She challenged opponents to beat her with odd-angled shots, and then, at the moment they had to decide where to place the ball, she faked them out. "I'm pretty

Briana's amazing jumping ability enabled her to reach balls more experienced goalkeepers could not.

instinctive," Briana says. "When people are shooting at me, I sense where they're going to aim. I go there, and it ends up looking like a brilliant save."

Briana was not a "textbook" goalie, but she was great at the one thing goalies must do—she kept the ball out of the net. Briana also remembers being the only African-American player on the field during most of her games. There were not many black families in her town, and soccer was not a sport that appealed to the black girls in her area. Although Briana can remember only a couple of times when an opponent made insulting racial remarks, she was always aware that she looked very different from the other girls on the field. "I was the fly in the milk," she says, half joking.

★ 3 ★

SOCCER WINS OUT

When it came time to start thinking about college, Briana assumed she would try for a basketball scholarship. But her final soccer season made her think differently. Briana was wonderful from the first game to the last. Anoka High made it to the state tournament, and Briana led the team to the finals. She played brilliantly in front of a roaring crowd in the Metrodome, and the Anoka Tornadoes were crowned champions of Minnesota. In 1990, Briana was named the top female athlete in the state.

Briana's coach encouraged her to talk to recruiters from colleges with top soccer programs. At first, she thought he was kidding. "I really didn't think I could get a scholarship," she says. "I didn't know how good I was."

The University of Massachusetts (UMass) knew how good Briana was, though. UMass coach Jim Rudy offered her a full scholarship and he told her how good he thought she could be. Although several schools were also recruiting Briana for basketball, she accepted the soccer scholarship from UMass. "I decided to focus on soccer after high school," she recalls, "because I figured I was a better goalkeeper than a basketball player, although I liked basketball better. I wanted to play basketball too, but my coach didn't really approve, so that was that."

Briana watched from the sidelines for a year, then as a sophomore established herself as the team's top goalie. She turned in a wonderful season in 1991—in the 19 games in which Briana played, she allowed just nine goals. Twelve times, she kept opponents from scoring a single goal.

Briana's college coach once said playing against her was like "rock-climbing a slab of marble."

After a save, strong-armed Briana always looks for an opportunity to start a play going the other way.

In 1993, UMass beat several top teams, including North Carolina, whose best player was the explosive scorer Mia Hamm. Briana was simply spectacular in this upset, which set the tone for the rest of the season. UMass rolled on to the Atlantic 10 championship, and Briana was named National Goalkeeper of the Year.

In the National Collegiate Athletic Association (NCAA) Tournament, the UMass Minutewomen made it all the way to the finals, before losing to North Carolina in a return match. Briana marveled at the skill of North Carolina's Tar Heels. Hamm was just awesome—faster than anyone on the field—and Kristine Lilly was the best passer she had ever seen. They, in turn, were impressed by Briana, who finished the year with 15 shutouts and ended her college career with a record of 48 wins, 13 losses, and 4 ties.

As good as Briana had become, she now knows she could have been even better. Quiet by nature, she didn't feel comfortable barking out instructions to her teammates. Instead, she would wait for a play to develop and just get ready to stop the shot. This put a lot of pressure on Briana, who often faced two dozen shots a game—a large number for a college goalkeeper. "I never spoke to anyone," she admits. "That's why I was making 20 to 25 saves a game." Only later did Briana discover that acting as a team's "traffic cop" is an important part of becoming a world-class goalie.

★ 4 ★

STARS IN STRIPES

During the Tar Heels' 1993 tournament win over UMass, North Carolina's coach, Anson Dorrance, watched as Briana faced an endless

barrage of shots in grim silence and with great determination. As an opposing coach, Dorrance was glad Briana did not shout instructions to her defenders. But he was also coach of the women's

Coach Anson Dorrance invited Briana to try out for the national team.

20

Former goalkeeper Tony DiCicco helped Briana polish her game after taking over as Team USA coach in 1994.

national team, and as such would never tolerate silence from one of his goalkeepers. Dorrance made this crystal clear in 1994, when he invited Briana to join Team USA.

As luck would have it, Briana joined Team USA just as Dorrance was leaving to devote himself to college coaching. His replacement, Tony DiCicco, a former goalkeeper, took a special interest in Briana's training. The team's starter, Mary Harvey, was battling injuries, so DiCicco knew he would have to give Briana a "crash course" in big-time soccer.

Whatever he did—it worked. In her first game, Briana overcame a case of the jitters and played well. "The first time I wore the Team USA jersey was in Portugal," she remembers. "I got very nervous, but [team captain] Carla Overbeck told me I belonged in the goal and that I belonged on the team. That made me feel awesome to hear her say that to me. I got a shutout my first game."

Confident and relaxed, Briana progressed rapidly. Practicing against former college foes Mia Hamm and Kristine Lilly—and the cannon blasts of superstar Michelle Akers—enabled Briana to learn something new every day. "The pressure they put on a goalie in practice is great preparation," she says. "When you've practiced against them, the game is actually easier. . . . Back home in Minnesota, my nephew and I stood in line to have a poster signed by Michelle," she marvels. "Now I'm on the same team with her!"

By the end of 1994, Briana's teammates were starting to call her "The Wall." Nothing got past her, and when she needed to make an impossible save, she almost always managed to pull it off. In August, Team USA won the prestigious Chiquita Cup and Briana was named the tournament's Most Valuable Player (MVP).

As a member of Team USA, Briana got to practice against some of the best players in the world.

In 1995, Briana was selected as Team USA's starter for the Women's World Cup, beating out Harvey and Saskia Webber, who had started under Coach Dorrance. Briana, under constant

Briana had a lot to think about after Team USA was eliminated from the 1995 World Cup. She has been almost perfect ever since.

★ ★ ★

Prior to the 1996 Olympics, the largest crowd
to attend a women's game in the United
es was about 6,000. That would change
ly, as more than 20,000 fans paid to see
USA thrash Denmark in the opening
Many of the television reporters covering
e had never seen a women's soccer
hey were in awe of Team USA's ability,
sports reports that evening featured
Team USA for the first time. Mia
e several highlight clips, and so
who played her usual solid game.
rnament moved forward, Team
ng invincible. The players had
d trained together for several
y played like the tight-knit
They got revenge on Norway,
rivals 2–1 in extra time,

on" during the 1996 Olympic game

attack, held up beautifully. She ma~
error during the tournament but ~
it was a costly one—the only go~
1–0 loss to Norway in the sem~
coming home with a gold m~
got the bronze.

Briana felt awful, but ~
know that everyone sh~
She had won 11 gam~
each one was a sh~
the credit for th~
not—they won ~
And from no~
lose a majc~

The n~
the 199~
for B~
of t~
b~

ever~
State~
quick~
Team ~
match. ~
the gam~
match. T~
and many ~
footage of ~
Hamm ma~
did Briana, ~
As the tou~
USA was feeli~
lived, eaten, an~
months, and the ~
group they were. ~
beating their arch~

Briana "rises to the occas~
against Norway.

Briana is in the middle of the celebration as the final whistle blows on Team USA's victory.

then defeated China in the final to win the gold medal. More than 75,000 people were in the stands that night, and the players really fed off the stadium's energy. Even Briana, by now famous for her stone-faced glare, sneaked a grin or two when she thought no one was looking. "The crowd was unbelievable," she says. "I couldn't help but smile."

The next major tournament came in 1998, at the Goodwill Games. Once again, the United States demolished its opponents and won the gold medal. All that remained for the "Triple Crown" of women's soccer was to capture the Women's World Cup, which was scheduled to be played in the United States in the summer of 1999.

★ 5 ★

CUP CRAZY

When Briana took the field at Giants Stadium in New Jersey for the opening match of the 1999 Women's World Cup, she could feel the energy of 78,972 noisy fans course through her body. Team USA's opponent, Denmark, never had a chance. Mia Hamm, Kristine Lilly, and cocaptain Julie Foudy scored beautiful goals, and Briana did not allow a shot to pass. It was her fiftieth career shutout.

Team USA advanced to the quarterfinals with a victory against North Korea. At this point, Briana had yet to be truly tested in the tournament. Little did she know that her

Briana keeps her eyes focused on the ball during a practice session right before Team USA will play Germany in the quarterfinals of the Women's World Cup.

greatest challenge would come from her own teammate. Early in the quarterfinal contest with Germany, Brandi Chastain attempted to boot the ball back to Briana, but put the ball in her own goal instead! Briana could have died right there.

Briana leaps high to snatch a ball away from an opponent during the World Cup semifinal game against Brazil.

The fact that President Bill Clinton and his family were at the game made the embarrassment even worse. It took great goals by Chastain and defender Joy Fawcett in the second half to dig Team USA out of its hole and score a 3–2 victory.

Now all that stood between Team USA and a trip to the World Cup final was Brazil. Six times during the game, Brazil hammered tough shots at Briana, and she saved every one. Briana's best save came on a shot that is almost an automatic goal. Brazilian striker Nene streaked unchecked down the right side and then launched a perfect ball toward the net from about 100 feet away. Briana resisted the temptation to step forward and leap for the shot, and instead took a step back before leaving her feet. She was just able to tip the ball over the bar. The look of disbelief on Nene's face told the whole story—Briana had made the save of the tournament. "That's got to be the best game I've ever played," Briana says of her performance in her team's 2–0 victory. "I was in the zone."

When the game ended, every member of Team USA sprinted toward the goal and mobbed Briana. She left the field pumping her fist in the air, as the crowd thundered its appreciation. "It felt good to have a game like that when the team needed me most," she says. "The fans definitely made a difference for me. Especially my parents, who finally got to a World Cup game. I'm very happy that I was able to do them proud."

Now Team USA had to deal with the Chinese team in the finals. The Chinese team had been improving steadily since it began competing in the late 1980s. More than 90,000 fans poured into the Rose Bowl in Pasadena, California, making it the largest crowd ever to witness a women's sporting event. Tony DiCicco was hoping to wear down China and score late in the game. DiCicco's counterpart, Ma Yuanan, instructed the Chinese players to tighten up on defense and wait for the Americans to get sloppy.

After regulation time expired, the game was scoreless. China, however, had gained an important advantage in the second half when Michelle Akers had to leave the field with an injury. Akers, Team USA's tallest player, was good at defending against corner kicks—a Chinese specialty.

Sure enough, in extra time, China executed a perfect corner kick. Briana watched helplessly as Fan Yunjie headed the ball toward the empty part of the net. But Kristine Lilly stepped in and blocked the shot at the last instant. As always, Kris was in the right place at the right time.

Extra time expired with the score still deadlocked at 0–0. The exhausted players lined up for a shootout to decide the championship of women's soccer. The focus now turned to Briana and Gao Hong, the Chinese goalie thought by many to be Briana's equal. Each team would send five players to blast penalty kicks from

12 yards out. The fans held their breath in anticipation as the shootout started.

Xie Huilin started by pounding a perfect shot to Briana's right, just beyond her reach. Team USA's Carla Overbeck scored to tie the shootout 1–1. Qiu Haiyan came right back and scored on Briana, but Joy Fawcett netted her attempt to keep Team USA even. China's third shooter, Liu Ying, seemed nervous and tired, and her face showed the strain of the intense pressure. As Liu approached the ball, something told Briana to go left. She took a step forward and then dove to the side—and blocked Liu's blast with her hands! The Rose Bowl exploded in cheers. "I read the kick pretty well," Briana recalls. "She hit it hard, but I don't think she placed it that well. I knew that I had to make one save. I knew my teammates would make their shots."

Briana's sprawling save against Liu Ying gave Team USA the chance it needed in the shootout against China.

That they did. Kristine Lilly and Mia Hamm made their shots, and then Brandi Chastain sealed Team USA's victory by kicking the ball past Gao. After five long years in goal, Briana finally was a world champion!

Briana rejoices after Brandi Chastain scores the goal that gives Team USA the 1999 Women's World Cup.

★ 6 ★

THINKING AHEAD, LOOKING BACK

Following its stunning victory, Team USA was the toast of the sports world—except in China. Chinese fans claimed that Briana had broken the rules by taking a small step forward before diving to the side on her Cup-winning save. In recent years, goalkeepers have not been whistled for this move, and it has become quite commonplace. In fact, Gao Hong had been guilty of the same infraction. "Their goalkeeper was stepping out," Briana confirms. "She just didn't save all of them, so no comment was made about her. Everybody does it."

The White House was one of the many stops Team USA made during their victory tour.

Briana's immense contribution to Team USA's victory made her an instant celebrity. In the weeks following the Women's World Cup, she agreed to do commercials for Pepsi and Allstate insurance, and appeared on the *Today Show*, *Good Morning America*, *Regis and Kathie Lee*, *Tonight with Jay Leno*, *The Late Show with David Letterman*, and *The Rosie O'Donnell Show*.

Between appearances, adoring fans mobbed her. "I was stopped everywhere," she marvels. "That's what it's like for the big guys. I never thought it would be me. It's crazy!"

Briana describes her famous save for *Tonight* show host Jay Leno. She became a talk-show regular after World Cup 1999.

"My life has changed a bunch," Briana continues. "I'm recognized wherever I go. Even if I don't have on my gear, people come up to me and shake my hand or ask for an autograph. There are times when it gets to be a bit much, but you can't deny the smiles on the kids' faces. That in itself makes it all worthwhile."

Back in 1989, when Briana made up her mind to give soccer everything she had, she never imagined that she would become one of the most famous athletes in her sport. It has meant placing her personal life on hold and putting aside her plans for a law career. Still, she does not regret a moment of her incredible journey.

"Soccer has been good to me," Briana maintains. "I can't complain. Teamwork, time management, leadership, and how to be successful are all things that will help me in my life after I'm done with the game."

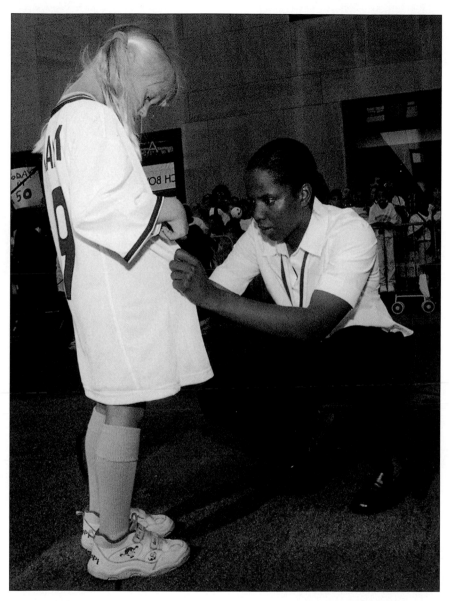

Briana signs a Team USA jersey for a young fan. She says that kids' smiles make the craziness of fame all worthwhile.

C ✦ H ✦ R ✦ O ✦ N

1971	• September 7: Briana is born in Dayton, Minnesota.
1982	• Briana joins her first organized soccer league.
1989	• Briana earns All-America honors after leading Anoka High School to the state title.
1990	• Briana is voted the top female athlete in Minnesota.
1991	• Briana becomes starting goalkeeper for UMass.
1992	• Briana starts three games at forward for UMass.

O ⋆ L ⋆ O ⋆ G ⋆ Y

1993 • Briana leads her school to the Final Four.
She is named NCAA Goalkeeper of the Year.

1994 • Briana joins Team USA and is named MVP
of the Chiquita Cup.

1996 • Briana helps Team USA win the gold medal
at the Summer Olympics.

1998 • Team USA wins the gold medal at the
Goodwill Games.

1999 • Briana saves the day for Team USA vs. China
in the Women's World Cup final.

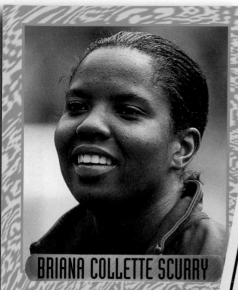

BRIANA COLLETTE SCURRY

Date of Birth **September 7, 1971**

Place of Birth **Dayton, Minnesota**

Height **5' 8"**

Weight **145 pounds**

High School **Anoka High School, Minnesota**

College **University of Massachusetts**

★ HONORS & CHAMPIONSHIPS ★

1989	High School All-American
1993	College All-American
	NCAA Goalkeeper of the Year
1996	Olympic Gold Medalist
1998	Goodwill Games Gold Medalist
1999	World Cup All-Star
	Women's World Cup Champion

ABOUT THE AUTHOR

Mark Stewart has written hundreds of features and more than fifty books about sports for young readers. A nationally syndicated columnist ("Mark My Words"), he lives and works in New Jersey. For Children's Press, Stewart is the author of more than twenty books in the Sports Stars series, including biographies of other women athletes, Lisa Leslie, Monica Seles, Marion Jones, and Mia Hamm. He is also the author of the Watts History of Sports, a six-volume history of auto racing, baseball, basketball, football, hockey, and soccer.